The local search series

Editor: Mrs Molly Harrison MBE

The Post Office

The local search series

Editor: Mrs Molly Harrison MBE

Many boys and girls enjoy doing research about special topics and adding drawings, photographs, tape-recordings and other kinds of evidence to the notes they make. We all learn best when we are doing things ourselves.

The books in this series are planned to help in this kind of 'project' work. They give basic information but also encourage the reader to find out other things; they answer some questions but ask many more; they suggest interesting things to do, interesting places to visit, and other books that can help readers to enjoy their finding out and to look more clearly at the world around them.

M.H.

Workers in a modern telephone exchange

The Post Office

Olive Royston BA

Line drawings by Margaret Carney

London Routledge & Kegan Paul

'. . . all the business of life is to endeavour to find out what you don't know by what you do'

John Whiting *Marching Song*

First published 1972
by Routledge and Kegan Paul Ltd
Broadway House, 68–74 Carter Lane, London, EC4V 5EL
Photoset and printed in Great Britain by
BAS Printers Limited, Wallop, Hampshire

ISBN 0 7100 7205 8 (C)
ISBN 0 7100 7206 6 (L)

Contents

		page
	Editor's preface	viii
1	Your project	1
2	The beginnings of the Post	5
3	Development of the Post in England	13
4	Postal services today	25
5	Other Post Office services today	36
6	Postage stamps	49
7	Post Offices	55
8	Post Office workers	63
9	The future	71
	Acknowledgments	74

Editor's preface

Everyone enjoys receiving letters, even if they do not like writing them, and people who have a telephone in their home are usually pleased when it rings. This is because most human beings do not like to be separate from others; they like to be in contact with other people, to 'keep in touch' as we say.
This book is about the biggest 'keeping in touch' organization there is – the Post Office Corporation. It is written to help you to look into many things that we often take for granted, and to find out what lies behind the postman who brings you letters and the men and women who sell you stamps. You may be surprised to learn how old the postal services are in this country; how simple they used to be and how very complicated they are now; and what a great deal of money and effort it all takes.
You will find suggestions for a lot of things to do, things to discuss and look out for, and things to make. And, who knows, this book might even give you the idea that you would enjoy working at one of the many jobs in the Post Office!

M.H.

Your project

1

What is the Post Office?

What does it do?

Your own project – planning and presentation

What is the Post Office?

Before you start work on your project about the Post Office, you need to think about what the Post Office really is. In the first place, of course, it is a building like the one you know near your home. In a wider sense, however, the Post Office means all the services the Post Office provides and even the whole organization concerned with these services. If you want to make your project a really good one, you will need to find out a good deal about the work of Post Offices as well as about what they look like.

What does it do?

How often do you visit a Post Office? – and why? It would be interesting to keep an account of this. You would probably find that you most often go to the Post Office to post a letter or to buy stamps. This is not surprising. If you make a list of all the other reasons why people might go to the Post Office, you will find that most of them have only been thought of in the last 100 years or so. On the other hand, the Post Office in England has been collecting and delivering letters for at least 400 years. Dealing with the 'mail' has always been a very important part of Post Office work, but in the past 100 years the Post Office has been doing a good many other jobs as well.

Your own project

If you are to make a good job of your project, it must be yours, not just other people's ideas put together or copied from books, though of course you will be able to get a good deal of information from reading and by asking questions, especially of people who work in the Post Office. So you will need a notebook, in which you can jot down your ideas, because when once you get really keen about your project you will find ideas may come to you at all sorts of odd times and may well be lost if you do not make at least a short note to remind you. A list of questions as they occur to you could go into the notebook, too, and you could tick them off when you have found the answers.

Illustrations

When you look at a book for the first time do you look at the pictures first? Most people do and it is easy to see why. A good clear picture tells a story or gives an idea which might otherwise need a page of writing. So illustrations will form a very important part of your project work and they can be of any kind that you are good at – sketches, paintings, photographs and so on. Another useful thing to do in your notebook will be to make lists of the illustrations you would like to have in your project – many of them will be a series. For example, you may decide it would be fun to keep a special look-out for different kinds of pillar-box – or postmen's uniforms – or Post Office vans and other vehicles of different dates – or Post Offices themselves and so on. You will be wise, too, to start straightaway to collect material for your illustrations. One section of your work, for instance, is sure to be about postage stamps, so you can begin to find out how to make a good collection of stamps – or pictures of them – if you do not already know. You are sure to collect a great many and you will have to decide later on which to use, so do not be in a hurry to mount them up.

Visits

Quite early on you will need to visit your local Post Office. You can make notes about what it looks like, why people go

Your local Post Office will supply a good deal of information for your project

there and what the clerks behind the counter have to do. Then you will be able to compare your Post Office with other larger or smaller ones you visit when you are on holiday, for instance. In this way you will feel that you are beginning to get to know for yourself about the Post Office. You will find, too, that there are a number of posters and other advertisements round the walls and some of these may well give you ideas. If there is a series of books of stamps displayed, you will notice that they contain much useful information, so you might think it worth while to collect and make use of different kinds of empty stamp-books.

Visits to museums may give you a good deal of help, especially if you live fairly near London or can visit it. In particular, there is a Post Office museum at Tottenham in north London, called the Bruce Castle Museum. The National Postal Museum just near St Paul's cathedral has most interesting displays of stamps. Many other museums, too, have displays of stamps and some show other things connected with the history of the Post Office. Be sure to check the opening times of the museum before you set out to visit it. Most museums sell pamphlets and postcards, but you should take along your own paper so that you can sketch just what you need, and of course you will have your notebook with you, too.

Planning your project

When you have a good deal of your information collected, you will need to work out a plan for your project – a number of headings or sections. And you will need to see that your work is well-balanced – that you have not made too much of some parts and not enough of others. This would make it lopsided and so much less interesting. A good way to check whether your work really is interesting is to look at it from someone else's point of view. For instance, would it be interesting to a foreigner or to a friend who does not know much about the Post Office?

Presentation

This is a most important part of your project because even a good piece of work can be quite spoilt if it does not look attractive. Any examiner will be put off by untidy, slovenly-looking work full of spelling mistakes. If you can type, it will be worth your while to find out if you are allowed to type your work. It would look neat and attractive. You should use double-spacing, which is easy to read. In any case, plan your margins carefully and also the spaces at the top and bottom of each page.

You will find it much easier to add something important after you have made a start, or to rearrange some parts of your project, if you use a loose-leaf system. You might think, too, whether it is worth while to write on only one side of the paper. Then you can put your illustrations in just the right places. When your work is finished, check very carefully to see that you have numbered your pages and your illustrations and that each illustration has a suitable caption to explain it.

You will find it useful to come back to these hints later on, but in the meantime in our first two chapters we will think about the writing and posting of letters in the past.

The beginnings of the Post 2

Early ways of sending messages

The first letters – how and why they were written

The first postmen

Official and private posts

The Royal Mail

Early ways of sending messages

Before the days of written letters, people communicated with each other by signals or symbols, especially in order to convey a message that was important to a whole group of people. For example, a quiver of arrows was sent as a declaration of war or a pipe as an offering of peace. Signal fires are still used by the aborigines in Australia. You have probably read how beacons were lit on hill-tops in England to spread important news and warnings, such as that of the sighting of the Spanish Armada off the coast in 1588. In some parts of the world messages are sent by the beating of drums. Which people have you heard about who use drums for sending messages? The Indians in Peru used to send messages by means of knotted cords of different lengths – each cord and each knot had a meaning.

If you decide to have a section in your project called something like, 'Sending messages before there were official postmen', it would be effective to have this section almost entirely in pictures.

On an outline map of the world you could mark the places mentioned in this chapter and then put in suitable pictures or symbols to show how messages were carried to and from each place in those early days.

The first letters – how and why they were written

Of course, the earliest letters were not written with a Biro on

sheets of paper. Do you know what was used instead? A visit to a museum, such as the British Museum in London, which has a section about life in ancient Egypt or Rome, would give you some of the answers. Or you could find out from books, such as John Robinson's *Looking at Language* in this Local Search Series. Some interesting illustrations of early letters might form a good introduction to your project.

Have you ever wondered how people first came to write letters? When travelling was very slow and difficult, some people felt the need to send messages to their friends or relatives who lived too far away for visiting to be possible. At first, of course, only very important messages could be sent in this way.

Sending letters

When you have written a letter today, it is a simple matter to send it on its way and even if it is going to the other side of the world – to New Zealand, for instance – you can feel pretty sure that it will be delivered there very soon after you post it. Perhaps you have taken this for granted. Just stop for a minute and think what actually happens. We shall discuss this more fully in a later chapter, but for the moment it is important to realize how little you have to do and how much other people do for you.

Three letter-carriers in early times

Before there was a regular postal service, anybody who wrote a letter had to find his own messenger to carry it for him. How would he set about this in those early times?

In some countries, including England, the king had to send messages to different parts of the country, so there were royal messengers. When the monasteries were very important, abbots had to write to one another from time to time; their messages were carried by lay-brothers. These were monks who had not taken the strictest vows and did not live all the time in a monastery. There were pedlars, too, who travelled about the country visiting the fairs where goods could be bought and sold. So, if you had to send a letter, you might ask either a royal messenger or a lay-brother or a pedlar to carry it for you.

These early letter-carriers were messengers rather than postmen. They took a letter the whole way from sender to receiver. In fact, they were rather like the famous Greek runners, who carried important messages and news either in their heads or written

on a clay tablet. Which was the more satisfactory way to carry a message?

Pigeons, too, have been used since very early times for carrying written messages. The Chinese used to roll a letter into a small cylinder and fasten it to a pigeon's middle tail feather. You may be able to think out why pigeons make good carriers.

The first postmen

Later on, when more letters were being sent, many of them over long distances, a kind of relay system gradually came into use. Each carrier had his own stretch of country to cover and then handed the letters on to the next man, as runners do in a relay race. This was when the words 'post', 'postman' and 'postboy' came into use. 'Post' comes from the Latin word *positus*, which means fixed. So when there were fixed places where a fresh carrier – or later a fresh horse – would be waiting to carry the mail over the next stage, these places became known as *posts*, and this name gradually came to mean the whole system of letter-carrying.

It was usual in early times for the messengers to carry a long pole, often with the letters fixed into a slit in its end. Only rich people sent letters, as a rule; the carriers were often servants. This method of carrying the letters meant that the messenger did not touch them. When diseases like plague were about, this was a wise precaution. If you are a Girl Guide or a Boy Scout, you will know that at one time Guides and Scouts carried poles. Do you know why? The real use of the messenger's pole was the same – for vaulting over ditches, puddles and streams.

In the early days, the postmen usually carried the letters in a leather bag called a *mail*. So you see where this word for letter-carrying has come from.

The first time that we hear of letters in England being carried on horseback is in 1481, when Edward IV set up relay-posts at intervals of twenty miles during his war against the Scots, but in other countries the mail had been carried on horseback much earlier than this. We know that Cyrus, the Persian emperor, set up stations at a day's ride from each other right across his empire in the sixth century B.C.

The most famous system for using horses in carrying the mail was that set up by the first Roman emperor, Augustus. His postmen were looked on as important people and were provided with good roads and fine horses. Later, chariots were used and the drivers wore a feather in their caps to show how swiftly they travelled. Perhaps you have heard people talk about something being a feather in someone's cap, and you can find out what this means. At the post stations along the Roman roads there were not only fresh horses and riders, but also supplies of fodder for the horses and equipment for shoeing them and for any repairs that might be necessary. Here, riders also could get refreshment.

You could sketch a piece of road and show the different kinds of letter-carriers – runners, pigeons, Persian and Roman horsemen and even Romans in chariots with feathers in their caps – where you think they would be along the road if they all set off together.

Official and private letters

It is important to remember that all the posts in early times were for official use only. In fact, private letter-writing was frowned on. Do you see why? Only a few men could write and the kings and emperors of the time were afraid that by writing to each other these men might plot to become too powerful.

Letters became very important for two other groups of people beside kings and abbots. Firstly, when the universities were set up in the Middle Ages, the students stayed there for several years and very seldom went home, so special messengers were used to carry letters backwards and forwards from the university cities to the homes of the students. Some of these special university messenger services were still in use at the beginning of the eighteenth century. If you can discover how students dressed in these early days of the universities, a sketch of one would be interesting.

Secondly, as towns grew up and trading developed between them, merchants needed to send more and more letters to each other and to their customers. By the sixteenth century, foreign merchants in London had set up their own service to carry messages to the Continent. Although the messengers often had to face storms and pirates when crossing the English Channel, this 'Strangers' Post', as it was called, became very important before it was abolished by Queen Elizabeth in 1591. A sketch of an Elizabethan merchant would make a good contrast to that of a university student, as both were among the earliest letter-writers.

The Paston Letters

Perhaps you have heard of these letters. They were written about 500 years ago by members of the Paston family, who lived in Norfolk. Nearly all the letters have been kept and of course they tell us a lot about what people did and thought then. It is also interesting to discover how they were sent. Usually this was by means of a servant or other messenger. Many of the letters say 'in haste'. This is almost certain to have been because a possible messenger had come along and could not be kept waiting too long.

From the Paston Letters we also know what a letter looked like then and how it was fastened together and addressed. It was made up of pieces of paper of various sizes all folded into an oblong packet about four inches long and two inches deep. A small hole was made in the letter, a piece of thread or thin cord was put through the hole, then the packet was securely sealed with wax. The seal covered the ends of the thread, so that it would be obvious if anyone tampered with the letter on the way. The address and the date of sending were written on the outside.

You might like to include an exact copy of one of the Paston Letters in your project, showing just what it looked like and explaining how it was sent on its journey and delivered at the other end.

Of course, delivering letters was not easy when houses had no numbers and even streets had no names. So you can guess what happened. The letter would be addressed to some well-known building and had to be called for there, just as you can still arrange to have your letters sent to your local Post Office 'to be called for' if this is more convenient than having them delivered.

The Royal Mail

In 1517, soon after the time of the Paston Letters, Henry VIII appointed Sir Brian Tuke to be the first Master of the Posts in England. A relay system was set up – like the earlier ones in Persia and Rome – with stages of ten to fifteen miles. This was the beginning of the Royal Mail and of course this name is still used for the post today. As you go around, it would be interesting to note down all the places where you see the words *Royal Mail.*

Dangers on the road

By the nineteenth century roads in England were better and conditions had become more settled. Earlier than this, letter-carrying in England was a very dangerous task. If you think of the dangers that postmen still face today in wilder parts of the world, you will know what some of these risks were – very cold or very hot weather, lightning, rivers in flood, wild animals and robbers. There was, too, the risk of losing their way, for there were very few signposts. A book published in 1664 says that one use of the postman's horn was to rouse the dogs in the nearest village, so that their barking would guide the postman. What other dangers can you think of? Here again a series of sketches would be very effective for your project.

Difficulties

In the early days of the Royal Mail, roads were often only rough tracks, dusty in summer and muddy in winter. There were often pot-holes in them, too. Perhaps you can think what might have been used to try to fill up these holes and whether this made matters better or worse.

Even when he had reached the end of his journey, the postman still had to find the people his letters were addressed to. In one case the address said: 'Tis fur old Mr Willey wot brinds de Baber in Langkaster ware te gal is. Gist rede him assune as it cums to ti Pushtufous.' Could you have delivered it, do you think? It scarcely looks like English, but in fact it means, 'Tis for old Mr Willey what prints the paper in Lancaster where the gaol is. Just read it to him as soon as it comes to the Post Office.'

Temptations

Nowadays postmen are better paid and we take it for granted that they will do their job honestly. In earlier times it was often a temptation to a postman to pocket the money paid in advance for carrying a letter and then to 'lose' the letter. Postmen could often make extra money 'on the side', too, by carrying private letters when they were not supposed to. Some postmen got into trouble for selling some of their equipment and we even hear of hungry postmen selling their trousers for food and then saying they had been robbed and asking for new ones. So there was a common saying at one time, 'crooked as a postman', and people often wrote threats to the postman on their letters. Oliver Cromwell wrote on a letter he posted in 1650: 'To our good Lord Dacre, Warden of the West Marshes, in haste; Haste, post, haste, for thy life, for thy life, for thy life.' Other people drew a skull and crossbones on their letters, or perhaps a man dangling from a gallows, as a threat to the postman.

In the next chapter we shall see how the Post in England gradually became better organized.

Development of the Post in England

3

Organizing the Post as a public service

Unofficial Posts

City Posts and country Posts

Mail coaches

Rowland Hill reforms the Post Office

Organizing the Post as a public service

At the end of the sixteenth century, there were only four regular post routes in England: London to Berwick, for Scotland; London to Holyhead, for Ireland; London to Dover and London to Plymouth, for other countries in Europe. You could mark these four routes in red, say, on an outline map of England and add later routes in other colours.

As well as the State Posts, there were a number of private carriers and it was Thomas Witherings, the Master of the Posts in the time of Charles I, who first organized the Post as a service for the public. He found the roads in a very bad state. Worse still, many of the posthouse keepers were in debt because their wages had not been paid. In fact, quite a number of them were so poor that they could not afford to keep horses and so the letters had to be carried on foot. Witherings set up new offices and new routes and fixed the charges for sending a letter.

In 1635 Charles I issued a proclamation, based on Witherings's reforms, which made it possible for anyone to send a letter by the postboys to almost any place in England and Wales, if they paid the postage rates Witherings had suggested.

The work of the postboys was to carry the mail from one office to another; the sender of a letter had to take it to a Post Office himself or send it by his own messenger, while at the other end of its journey the letter was kept at the Post Office until it was claimed.

Sir Brian Tuke, the first Master of the Posts in England, 16th century

Colonel Henry Bishop, Post Master General, 17th century

John Bunyan, who wrote *Pilgrim's Progress*, also wrote this:

On The Post-Boy

Behold this Post-boy, with what haste and speed
He travels on the Road; and there is need
That he so does, his Business call for haste.
For should he in his Journey now be cast,
His Life for that default might hap to go;
Yea, and the Kingdom come to ruin too.
Stages are for him fixt, his hour is set,
He has a Horn to sound, that none may let
Him in his haste, or give him stop or stay.
Then Post-boy blow thy horn, and go thy way.

In Cobham in Surrey, there is a street called Postboys' Row. You could keep a look-out for others and perhaps sketch them. Despite the name, the postboys, of course, were men.
One interesting rule at this time was that when a Mail arrived in London from the Continent the letters for the King and his Ministers had to be delivered first. After that, a list of all other

Ralph Allen, Postmaster in Bath, 18th century

Sir Rowland Hill, 19th century

letters was put up in the office 'for every man to view and demand his letters'. You could make a picture in coloured paper, or material, showing the postmaster walking away after putting up the list, and some of the recipients opening their letters.

Unofficial Posts

For some time after the establishment of a public Post, other companies of carriers were still allowed to carry letters over routes not served by the official Post. These companies carried goods and passengers, as well as letters. Over 200 routes are listed in the 'Carriers' Cosmography' (or timetable) for 1637. Here are two entries from the list:

1 The Carriers of Banbury in Oxfordshire doe lodge at the George neere Holborne bridge, they goe and come wednesdaies, thursdaies and fridaies.

2 The Carriers of Manchester doe lodge at the two-neck'd Swan in Lad lane (between great Woodstreet and Milk-street end), they come every thursday.

MAIL ROUTES
AND
POST TOWNS
ORGANISED BY
THOS. WITHERINGS
1635–51
EDDINBURGH
Haddington
Cockburnspath
Berwick
Belford
Alnwick
Morpeth
NEWCASTLE
Durham
Carlisle
Penrith
Brough
Greatabrigg
Richmond
Darlington
Northallerton
Whitby
Scarbrough
Bridlington
Kendal
Lancaster
Borrowbridge
YORKE
Skipton
Wetherby
Tadcaster
Leeds
Bradford
Wakefield
Howden
HULL
Ferribrigge
Preston
Ormskirke
Liverpool
Warrington
Manchester
Stopport
Doncaster
Grimsby
Gainsbrough
Louth
Sheffield
Bawtry
Tuxford
Lincoln
Alford
Wainfleet
Holyhead
Beaumoris
Conway
Denbigh
Northop
CHESTER
Knutsford
Macclesfield
Cogerton
Chesterfield
NEWARK
Nampwich
Brereton Green
Ashbourn
Wrexham
Uttoxeter
Stone
Nottingham
Grantham
Boston
Witchurch
Drayton
Derby
Stafford
Loughboro
Post Wittam
SHREWSBURY
Welshpoole
Shifnal
Litchfield
Leicester
Peterborough
Wisbech
Lynn
Wells
Walsingham
Fakenham
Swaffham
Walsham
Alesham
Norwich
YARMOUTH
Windham
Attleborough
Downham
Beckles
Southwold
Thetford
Aberdovy
Mahuntleth
Teanedomine
Wolverhampton
BIRMINGHAM
Colshall
Harbrough
Stylton
Ely
Stourbridge
Kidderminster
Coventry
Huntingdon
Ludlow
Bewdly
Bromsgrove
Droitwich
Warwick
Daventry
Wellingbrough
Caxton
Newmarket
Bury
Saxmundham
Tenbury
Strat-upon Avon
Northampton
Cambridge
Lavenham
Milford
Ipswich
Aldborough
Worcester
Evesholme
Towcester
Bedford
ROISTON
Weldon
Sudbury
Cardigan
Landovey
Hay
Hereford
Morttenhinmarsh
Banbury
Brickhill
Thaxted
Harwich
Brecknock
Brodway
Buckingham
Dunstaple
Ware
Dunmow
Braintree
Colchester
Carmarthen
Monmouth
Gloucester
Witham
Kelden
Pembrook
Burford
Oxford
Alesbury
St. Albans
Chelmesford
Waltham
Maldon
Lechlade
Abington
Barnet
Uske
Cirencester
Farrington
Nettlebed
Ingerstone
Burntwood
Rumford
Swansea
Hounslow
Maidenhead
Gravesend
Shereness
Thanet
Cardiffe
BRISTOLL
Chippenham
Newberry
Windsor
Dartford
Reading
Staines
Chepstead
Rochester
Sittingbourn
Faversham
Bath
Marlebrough
Hartford
Kingston Bridge
Seavenock
Maidstone
Canterbury
Deale
Trowbridge
Devizes
Sandwich
Froom
Westbury
Basingstoke
Gullford
Tonbridge
Ashford
Warminster
DOVER
Wells
Andover
Alton
Godliman
Minehead
Dunster
Bridgewater
Winchester
Haslemere
Stonecrouch
Salisbury
Midhurst
Sommerton
Ilchester
Evill
Petworth
Rye
Barnstaple
Taunton
Petersfield
Arundell
Hastings
Shasbury
Tiverton
Chard
Sherbourn
Southampton
Biddeford
Crookhorn
Chichester
Honniton
Blandford
PORTSMOUTH
EXETER
Axminster
Poole
Isle of Wight
Lyme
Dorchester
Launston
Weymouth
Ashburton
Padstow
Totnesse
Fowy
Loo
PLYMOUTH
Dartmouth
Truro
Market Jew (Penzance)
Falmouth

City Posts

By about the year 1650, important cities like Amsterdam, London and Paris were linked by some kind of postal service with most of the important places in the world at that time. Yet in 1665 only forty-five people worked in the Post Office in London. Thirty of them died in the bad outbreak of plague that year. It was not until 1680 that any postal service was set up in London itself. Then two Londoners, Robert Murray and William Dockwra, arranged to collect and deliver letters there for a fee of one penny. Other cities soon followed London's example.

Country Posts

Although a regular postal service had been set up along the main roads between the chief towns and later in the largest towns themselves, yet the service remained very poor in country districts and the smaller towns. This was partly remedied by Ralph Allen, a postmaster in Bath in 1715. He started a system of 'cross-roads Posts'. Before this, letters between places only a few miles apart had to travel up to London, out along one of the main roads, then along a side road. This of course was many miles further than the distance between the two places and took an absurdly long time. It would be interesting to draw a map of the six 'A' roads out of London, mark in two places not on any of them and then join the two places with a line in one colour. Then in another colour you could show how a letter would have travelled from one place to the other before Allen's cross-roads Posts.

Allen also found that postboys on the cross-roads often dawdled, went out of their way to oblige some private person – and of course got paid for it – and wasted a lot of time visiting inns and kitchens on their way. He set to work to prevent these dishonest practices in his district. How would you have set about it, do you think? He kept careful lists of all the letters and the money paid for them. He also checked and inspected the work of the postboys. In this way, he speeded up the delivery of letters. He set up new routes in his area, too. He was so successful that he was asked to organize the Post in other districts too, and so he became very rich. It is pleasing to know that he gave a great deal of his money to charity.

In Allen's time, and for many years afterwards, people who lived in the country still had to fetch their letters from the nearest Post Office or pay an extra fee to the postmaster to have them delivered.

Post coaches

The first wheeled passenger vehicles appeared on the roads of England in the fifteenth century. They were very heavy and clumsy and had no springs at all. You can imagine what a coach journey was like then, even for an inside passenger. The postmen travelled outside and were even more uncomfortable. Gradually coaches became lighter and more comfortable; those carrying the Mail were called Post coaches. Because accidents and robbery were so common, it was quite usual at this time for passengers to make their wills before setting out on a journey by Post.

John Palmer, the owner of a theatre in the fashionable city of Bath in the eighteenth century, found that, 'The mail was entrusted to some idle boy without character, mounted on a worn-out hack, who so far from being able to defend himself against a robber, was more likely to be in league with one.' By this time, private coaches were forbidden to carry mails,

One of the early Mail coaches.

but actually they often carried more letters than the official Post did, because they were cheaper. The official charge for a long-distance letter to London was eight pence, but people soon found that they could pay the driver of a private coach a penny or two, and another penny so that he would drop the letter into Dockwra's city Post when he reached London.

John Palmer was energetic and full of ideas and he wondered why the Post should not set up a network of coaches, swifter and better equipped than the private ones, and so give a better service than anyone else. He soon produced a detailed plan to show how this could be done.

Palmer's Mail coaches

Palmer's plan met with a good deal of opposition, but he was supported by the Prime Minister, William Pitt, with the result that on 2 August 1784 a specially built coach was sent on an experimental run from Bristol to London. People lined the roads and cheered it on its way. Great enthusiasm was aroused when it was found, on arrival in London, that the coach had travelled at an average speed of over seven miles an hour, in spite of stops on the way.

After this, John Palmer was made Comptroller General of the Post and by 1790 he had Mail coaches operating all over Britain. New roads were built and existing ones improved, so that before long the Mail coaches were travelling at ten miles per hour, to the consternation of many people of the time who thought this a very dangerous speed. This meant, for example, that the journey from London to Edinburgh took three nights and two days, instead of six days and nights.

Efficiency was Palmer's aim. For him, the speed and reliability of the Mails came first. At relay-inns the horses were changed in less than a minute. When the coach stopped for meals, unpunctual passengers were simply left behind. Palmer's coaches carried an armed guard as well as a coachman. The guard sat at the back of the coach with his feet on the locked lid of the boot containing the mail, his blunderbuss and pistols in front of him and his horn beside him. No one was allowed to sit behind him or above him. Because he was employed by the Post Office, the guard had a special uniform. At the end of the eighteenth century he wore a scarlet cloth coat with blue lapels, blue linings, blue waistcoat and a hat with a gold band. A coloured sketch of one of these guards would look well in your project. As Palmer had anticipated, the presence of an armed guard soon put a stop to the robbing of mail coaches.

The coaches travelled so fast that we hear that the coachman and guard were sometimes 'chucked from their seats'. Except at relay-stations, the Mail was loaded and unloaded without stopping. A further aid to speed was the guard's horn. He used this to announce in advance the arrival of the Mail coach at inns and toll-gates and to warn other traffic to give way. Sometimes the guard might play a tune on his horn. If he met another coach which was late he would very likely play, 'Oh dear, what can the matter be?' as they dashed past each other. Palmer's Mail coaches were so punctual that people got into the habit of setting their clocks and watches by them.

An early railway

In 1825, however, a completely new way of travelling was started in England – the railway started to rival the roadway. See if you can find out which two towns the first railway ran between. The last stage coach ran in 1846. So in twenty-one years the railway had completely killed the stage coach.

Rowland Hill and the Penny Post

Rowland Hill, one of the best-known men in Post Office history, was born in 1795. Although he was not employed by the Post Office at that time, he published a pamphlet in 1836 called *Post Office Reform: Its Importance and Practicability*. He was the first person who believed that the purpose of the Post was to serve everybody rather than to make money.

In his pamphlet he pointed out what he thought was wrong with the Post and how it could be set right. For instance, the fee for sending a letter was far too high for poorer people. When the poet Coleridge was walking one day in the Lake District, he saw a postman stop at a cottage and offer a letter to an elderly woman. She turned it over and then handed it back to the postman. The letter was from her son, but she could not afford to pay the fee. Coleridge offered to pay for the letter, but the woman would not let him and when the postman had gone she told Coleridge that there was no writing inside the letter. She said her son regularly sent her letters like that. From the way in which he spaced and wrote the address, she could tell how he was getting on.

While poorer people could not afford to send letters at all, certain important people enjoyed the privilege of 'franking'. (This word comes from a Latin word meaning free.) People like the royal family, ambassadors, cabinet ministers, church officials and other people of high rank, as well as postal officials, had the right to send mail free of charge. It was quite common, too, for these people to frank letters for their friends and relations, who were not entitled to this privilege, so, as Rowland Hill pointed out, the whole system was most unfair. You could mention the people to whom we can send a letter free of charge today and say what we must write on the envelope to show that we are allowed to do this.

Rowland Hill also pointed out that the distance a letter travelled made very little difference to the cost of sending it. The handling of the letter, rather than the carrying, was the expensive part. By this time, every letter was handed to a postal clerk, who examined it to see where it was going to and then wrote down the postage due. He also kept an account-book, in which he noted down the amount of the fee to be collected by the postman. Then the letter went to other clerks, who, if there was any doubt, checked whether the letter was written on one sheet of paper or more, because the fee depended on how many sheets of paper there were. At the other end, as we have seen, the postman had to deliver the letter himself and collect the fee.

TO ALL POSTMASTERS
AND
SUB-POSTMASTERS.

GENERAL POST OFFICE,
25th April, 1840.

It has been decided that Postage Stamps are to be brought into use forthwith, and as it will be necessary that every such Stamp should be cancelled at the Post Office or Sub-Post Office where the Letter bearing the same may be posted, I herewith forward, for your use, an *Obliterating Stamp*, with which you will efface the Postage Stamp upon every Letter despatched from your Office. *Red Composition* must be used for this purpose, and I annex directions for making it, with an Impression of the Stamp.

As the Stamps will come into operation by the *6th of May*, I must desire you will not fail to provide yourself with the necessary supply of Red Composition by that time.

Directions for Preparing the Red Stamping Composition.

1 lb. Printer's Red Ink.
1 Pint Linseed Oil.
Half-pint of the Droppings of Sweet Oil.
To be well mixed.

By Command,

W. L. MABERLY,
SECRETARY.

An important official notice of 1840

So in February 1837, Rowland Hill published these proposals:

1 that the postal rate should be so low that everyone could afford to send and receive letters.
2 the rate should be the same for all places in England.
3 the rate should depend on the weight of the letter and not on how many sheets of paper it contained.
4 the rate for the minimum weight should be one penny.
5 all letters should be paid for in advance. (This saved a great deal of money.)

An Act of Parliament, passed in 1838, included all these proposals and also abolished franking. For a time, a letter weighing half an ounce was to cost fourpence, but on 10 January 1840, the Penny Post was introduced. Here is part of the Post Office Regulations about it:

> On and after the 10th January, a letter not exceeding half an ounce in weight, may be sent from any part of the United Kingdom, to any other part, for One Penny, if paid when posted, or for Twopence if paid when delivered.

Rowland Hill made two other important suggestions:

1 the use of what he called pre-payment wrappers.
2 the use of postage stamps.

He described a stamp as a bit of paper just large enough to bear the stamp and covered at the back with a glutinous wash'. This meant, of course, that the paper was to be stamped in ink and gummed.
In the early part of the nineteenth century, the London letter-carrier wore a uniform very much like that of the guard of the Mail coach, but in 1861 Rowland Hill introduced a blue uniform with red pipings, very much like the modern postman's.

Speeding the Mail

On land the Post was sent more quickly by using, first, horses, then coaches and finally railways. Foreign Mail has been speeded

A stamp illustrating the speeding-up of overseas mail

up by using ships driven by steam and oil instead of only by wind, and in modern times, aeroplanes.

I expect you have made time-charts in your history lessons, or seen them in books. A good way to show clearly what the chief improvements in sending the Mail were, would be to make time-charts, one for carrying the inland mail and another for foreign mail. You could do this with words and colours, but it would be much more interesting to use symbols for each method of transport. Your history teacher would discuss this with you.

Postal services today 4

The Post in modern times

Collecting, sorting, transporting and delivering letters

Speeding the mail

Some special kinds of letters and packets

The Post in modern times

Have you any idea how many letters are posted in Britain every day? Thousands? No, millions. In fact, more than thirty million. If you try to imagine all these letters piled up on top of one another, the pile would be four times the height of Mount Everest, the highest mountain in the world. As well as this, more than 600,000 parcels are sent each day. So you see that the Post Office handles an enormous amount of business.

In fact, it employs more men and women than anyone else in the country.

You might be interested to get exact figures and make a coloured diagram to compare the number of people who work for the Post Office with the numbers that work for the Coal Board, British Rail, the Electricity Board and the Gas Board. You might be able to get the figures from your local library or you could ask at the local offices of these Boards.

Collecting the letters

Have you ever wondered how people posted their letters before there were pillar-boxes? In the time of Queen Anne (1702–14), a man called Charles Povey set up a foot-post in London. He employed collectors 'to go about the streets ringing bells' to let people know they could bring out any letters they wanted to post. These men came to be called bellmen. They carried

When and where might you have seen this bellman?

a locked bag with a slit for the letters and usually went around collecting letters in the late afternoon, so that they could deliver the letters to the Mail coaches before they set out on their journeys. Bellmen collected the letters in London and other large towns for over 100 years. Perhaps you could find out whether bellmen ever collected the mail in the towns near your home. They were abolished in 1846.

The earliest London pillar-boxes were four-sided, although the very first ones, set up in the island of Jersey in 1852, were six-sided. All the early pillar-boxes were made of iron. What are modern ones made of? They have not changed very much in size. Notice their shape. By 1857, pillar-boxes were being placed at the side of country roads as well as along the streets in towns. In the same way as the bellmen arranged the times of their collections to fit in with the times of the Mail coaches, the collections from the new pillar-boxes were timed to fit in with the trains which carried the main mails, and of course this still happens.

Today, however, there is an army of over 110,000 postmen to deal with the vast numbers of letters and parcels now sent through the Post in Britain.

Sorting

All this mail is taken to the local sorting offices. Do you know what happens to it there? To begin with, there are three jobs to be done – segregating, facing-up and cancelling. Segregating means separating one kind of letter or packet from another and this takes place in two stages. First, packets are separated from letters. Do you see why this needs to be done? Imagine a packet containing a piece of wedding-cake, for example. Such packets have to be stamped by hand, because they are too bulky and probably too fragile to go through the stamp-cancelling machine. Then smaller letters are sorted from larger ones. Later on, they will be put into receptacles of two different sizes.

Facing-up means arranging the letters so that their stamps are all in the same position. This makes it easy to cancel the stamps by machine. Letters pass through the stamp-cancelling machine at the rate of six hundred a minute. If you get a pile of real or

Two of London's earliest pillar boxes. Where were the letters posted?

imaginary letters and see how many stamps you can cancel in a minute, you will get some idea of how much time these machines save.

The next step is what the postman calls 'outward sorting'. This means sorting out the letters according to their destinations. The postman puts each letter into one of forty-eight pigeon-holes. Can you think why there should be this number and not more or less? Picture to yourself how far a postman can reach without moving from the spot. The letters for one county, or perhaps two or three small ones, or for one city or town, are put into the same pigeon-hole. In the case of large towns like London, there will have to be a second sorting later on. You will realize that the main problem facing the sorter is to sort out a large amount of mail as quickly as possible. Perhaps you have noticed in your Post Office notices about the correct way to address letters. If you thought these notices were not necessary, you would change your mind if you were the postman sorting out all the letters. You will realize, too, how much it helps if people address their letters in clear handwriting or typing.

Transporting the mail

The letters from each pigeon-hole are tied into bundles and put into mail-bags. Full mail-bags are sent direct to the sorting office for the particular town or district where the letters are to be delivered. When there are not so many letters for one place, the mail-bags from several sorting offices may be collected at one office and the letters from all the mail-bags transferred to one or two bags. Finally, the mail-bags are sent to the nearest railway station or taken the whole way by road or perhaps air.

It would be worth your while to arrange to visit your local sorting office, so that you could actually see what goes on there. This would give you a much clearer picture of it. You could notice, for example, how the forty-eight pigeon-holes are arranged.

Mail trains

A great many mail trains travel by night, so that it will not be so

The exterior of a very early travelling Post Office coach. What happened to the bag of mail and what was the purpose of the net?

Interior of a travelling Post Office carriage in about 1900

easy for you to find out at first hand what happens on them, but there is a very good documentary film called *30 Million Letters* that you might get the chance to see.

Until the year 1971, a special kind of apparatus was placed close to the railway line at certain points. This collected mail thrown out of the train and delivered other mail to the train, as it continued on its journey at full speed. Some of the mail trains are fitted up as travelling Post Offices, so that before the train reaches its destination the postmen on board have sorted out the mail still further. In this way its delivery at the other end is as speedy as possible. The idea of travelling Post Offices was first

introduced in 1838 on the Grand Junction Railway connecting Birmingham, Manchester and Liverpool. Did you know that in America there have been experiments with delivering the mail by rocket carriers?

London's underground railway

Because of its size, London has the only underground Post Office railway in the world. This was planned in 1913, but, because of the First World War, did not come into use until 1927. It runs from Paddington in the west to Whitechapel in the east, with intermediate stops at Britain's largest sorting office – do you know the name of this? – at the King Edward Building of the Post Office which is in the City, and at Liverpool Street station.

Loading containers onto a train on the Post Office railway at Mount Pleasant. Notice the possible destinations of the train

You could find these stations on a map of London and make your own map of this railway. The underground tubes are nine feet across and each has two lines of track. The trains travel at forty miles an hour and there is a train every four minutes. The most interesting fact about this railway is that there are no drivers; the trains are operated by remote control. You could make a list of ways in which it is an advantage to have this railway. Think how the mail would otherwise have to be carried, of its enormous bulk, the number of extra postmen that would be needed . . . and what else?

Other methods of transporting the mail

If you have been keeping a watch for everything with Royal Mail on it, you are sure to have seen motor vans and motor-cycles. Pictures of an early mail-van drawn by horses, and of a modern one, would make this part of your project interesting. You might find it interesting, too, to make a list of the kings and queens from 1900 to today and then see if you can find and draw their 'ciphers' from mail-vans or from pictures of them. If you have found different ciphers on pillar-boxes or elsewhere, you could draw these as well.

One of the first motor mail vans. Before 1905, mail vans belonged to private people, who rented them to the Post Office. Notice the Post Office and the postmen's uniforms

Delivering the mail

At the end of its journey, a letter again arrives at a sorting office in a mail-bag from the railway station or mail van. This time the letters are sorted into pigeon-holes, each of which holds letters for one part of the town or district. Sometimes the letters in one pigeon-hole will all be delivered by one postman, but very often there will be another sorting into the rounds for two or three postmen. Before he sets out on his actual delivery round, the postman will arrange his letters in the order in which he will deliver them. He calls this 'setting-in'.

A model of a sorting office, to show the beginning and end of a letter's journey, as it were, would be most effective in your project. You would need to visit at least one sorting office, of course, to be sure that you get the details right.

Modern ways of speeding up the mail

For a long time, as we have seen, the postman had to deliver his letters himself, but in 1837 Rowland Hill suggested a completely new idea – that house letter-boxes would speed up the delivery of the mail. So people began to have slits cut in their front doors for this purpose. Perhaps you could find and sketch an eighteenth-century door which has had a letter-box added in the nineteenth century.

Then, too, pillar-boxes in streets or out in the country save people a great many journeys to the Post Office.

The first machine for cancelling stamps was invented by Rowland Hill's son, Pearson, in 1857. Today special machines can segregate, face and cancel letters automatically. In some sorting offices, moving belts and conveyors save time and energy, while electronic machines for sorting letters and parcels are used in some of the larger offices.

You could make an interesting series of drawings of labour-saving devices used by the Post Office.

In London from 1856 onwards, the mail was delivered more quickly because of another of Rowland Hill's ideas. This was to divide London into ten postal districts and give each of them a name according to its position. Letters standing for these names were put after London on letters, and so made sorting simpler and quicker. Most of these postal districts are still in existence today – East Central, West Central, North, South-West and so on. In 1917 each district was divided up into a number of sub-districts and each of these had a number. Until recently, the address on a London letter ended with something like LONDON, S.E.4. This again helped to simplify the sorting of the enormous number of letters that reached London each day, because it was much quicker to read these letters and figures than the whole name of the district. Several other large cities had a similar system.

A system of 'Post Codes' is gradually being introduced. At first sight these are very complicated, but coding-desk operators in the sorting offices turn them into phosphorescent marks that can be 'read' by machines, so that this is yet another device for making sorting quicker.

Air mail

Sending foreign mail by air has, of course, speeded up the service enormously. In 1911, at the time of the coronation of George V, a special air-mail service was introduced. It was between Hendon, the only important air-base at that time, and Windsor. The letters had the postmark, 'First United Kingdom Aerial Post'. After this, air-mail services to the colonies and to France were set up. In 1919, letters could travel by air from London to Paris for two shillings and sixpence per ounce; by about ten years later, this charge had been reduced to twopence per ounce. Nowadays, of course, there are regular and frequent air-mail services to most parts of the world and the cost is often little more than that of sending a letter in this country.

The first United Kingdom Aerial Post, 1911. Notice the position of the mail bags

Special kinds of letters

There are special ways of sending urgent or important or valuable letters. Find out what a registered letter is, and what is meant by Recorded Delivery. You could show receipts for these two kinds of special letters and explain when you would use them.

'Express' letters can be sent between Britain and other countries. What do you think people do now instead of sending an express letter to someone else in Britain? How is this better?

You can find out at your Post Office about these and other special ways of sending letters, or you can ask at your local library if you may look at a copy of the Post Office Guide.

Foreign letters

These can usually be sent either by sea or by air. You could find out exactly what you have to do in each case. Which is quicker and so more expensive? You could include a printed air letter in your work and explain how it is different from an envelope.

Post cards

These came into use in 1870 and the postage was only half as much as for a letter. Since 1968, however, it has cost the same to send a postcard as a letter, but I expect you can think of a special kind of postcard that people still like to send. You could mount one in your work.

Lost letters

We occasionally hear of a letter being delivered some years after it was posted or even not being delivered at all. Lost letters are sent to the Dead Letter Office in London and there they are opened and, if possible, returned to the sender. This, of course, is why it is so important to put the address at the top of our letters.

Parcels

You could explain why parcels are usually posted at a Post

Loading the Christmas mail for Australia at Tilbury Docks

Office rather than in a pillar-box and why they are kept separate from letters. If you are good at outline sketches, you could show, perhaps in an amusing way, some of the things that might happen to the letters – or the parcels – if they travelled together. Parcels for abroad have to have a Customs Declaration label stuck on the outside. You fill in the label to say what is in the parcel, so that if there is a tax on it in the country the parcel is going to, the Customs officials there will know about it without opening the parcel. You could get one of these labels and fill it in for an imaginary parcel you are sending abroad and explain why the label is necessary.

There are also new postal services such as 'Datapost', and you might like to find out what these are, and how they operate.

5 Other Post Office services today

Quicker communication by telegram and telephone

Growth of the British telephone system

Telex

Radio and television

The collection, transporting and delivering of written letters is still, of course, a very important part of the work of the Post Office. Now, however, there is also a department of 'telecommunications' for dealing with quicker modern methods of sending messages. The use of these newer methods has grown very rapidly in the 100 years since they were first introduced. Telegrams came first, then telephones and later still radio and television. If you know the meaning of 'tele-', you will see that their names imply quick communication over long distances.
The rapid growth of telecommunications in the past 100 years will probably be best shown in your project by graphs and charts. Your maths teacher and your history teacher would help you. For example, it would be effective to make a time-chart showing the inventions being used by people dressed in contemporary costume.

Telegrams

If you have never sent a 'wire', you could find out at the Post Office how it is done and how much it costs. Telegrams can also be sent by telephone. How is this an advantage? How is the message sent on from the Post Office? You could make sketches to show the whole journey of a telegram from your home to your friend's home. A Greetings telegram and an ordinary one displayed side by side would look well, too.
In 1868 a Bill was presented to Parliament 'to enable the

The first mobile Telegraph Office, used in March 1872 at the Oxford and Cambridge boat race

A Wheatstone telegraph, invented in 1840 and used until after 1900. A message could be sent by turning the handle and pressing the buttons opposite the right letters or figures on the lower dial. Messages were received by writing down the letters the pointer stopped at in the top dial

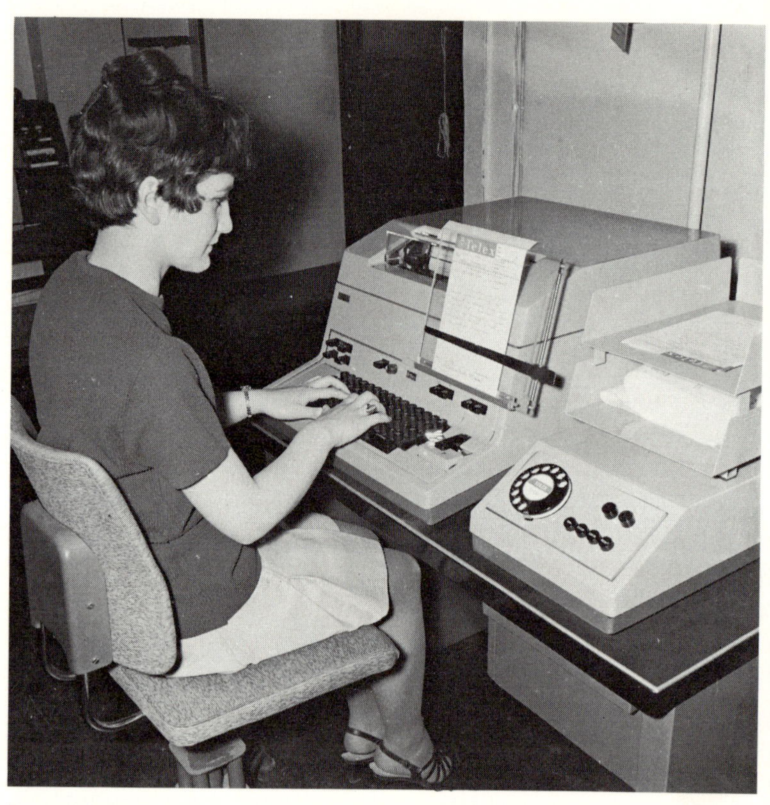

Teleprinter with automatic transmitting facilities

Post-Master General to acquire, work and maintain electric telegraphs' and a year later another Act of Parliament gave the Post Office a monopoly of telegraph business.

You may perhaps have learnt to send messages with semaphore flags or in the Morse code of dots and dashes. Both these methods were used for sending telegraph messages before electricity came into use. At first, Semaphore was used. The Admiralty in London used to send code messages to the Naval Dockyard at Portsmouth in this way. This is a distance of seventy miles, so you can work out what was used instead of a person with a flag in each hand. The old-fashioned kind of railway signals would give you the idea. The last Semaphore message from London to Portsmouth was sent in 1847. After that, Morse was used.

You could sketch someone signalling with Semaphore flags, and also tapping in Morse. It would be interesting, too, to write out a message in Morse and put the letters under each of the Morse signs. You could explain that the teleprinter is now used for inland telegrams – and perhaps include a picture of one. The Morse code is still used for sending messages to ships at sea. Perhaps you could get a picture of Samuel Morse and write a little about him.

This is what Queen Victoria wrote in her Journal on 9 July 1851: 'We went to the Exhibition and had the electric telegraph show explained and demonstrated before us. It is the most wonderful thing, and the boy who worked it does so with the greatest ease and rapidity.'

In the same year, the first under-water telegraph cable was laid between England and France. In 1858, a cable was laid under the Atlantic Ocean from Ireland to Newfoundland, and Queen Victoria and President Buchanan of the United States exchanged messages.

By the end of the 1920s, 'wires' were being sent by wireless over long distances. For example, a wire could be sent from Britain to Canada for 1½d. per word. Perhaps you could find out how the message was sent from the Post Office to the radio station.

Telephones

Sending a telegram is quicker than writing a letter, especially if the wire is sent 'reply paid', so that the recipient can send his answer straight away, but, of course, it is quicker still to use the telephone. You could make a list of the many advantages of the telephone – plans can be discussed and settled immediately, busy people like doctors can connect their phone to a tape-recording which tells callers how to get help . . . what else?

Simple telephones

The forerunner of the telephone was the speaking-tube. Perhaps you have seen one in use in a shop or factory, for speaking to someone in the same building. You could make a very simple telephone yourself. You need two tins joined by a piece of string and also a friend to help you. If the string is pulled very tight, when you speak into one tin, your friend – in the next room, perhaps – will be able to hear faintly what you are saying if he puts his ear to the other tin. If you have learnt about sound-waves in your science lessons, you will understand that the tight string carries the sound-waves from one tin to the other. Perhaps your science teacher would explain to you how to construct a more efficient telephone, using an electric battery.

The British telephone system

Here are two impressions of the early telephone, this from *Punch* in 1877:

> On putting the instrument to my ear, I felt somewhat as if a regiment of the line had fired a volley, at a hundred yards, into that member.

and this from *The Times* in 1879:

> By its means the human voice can be conveyed in full force from any one point to any other five miles off, and with some loss of power to a very much more considerable distance still.

One of the first small telephone exchanges set up in the parlour of the operator's home

At this time, telephones belonged to private companies. You could find out why one of them was called the Edison Telephone Company and include a picture of Thomas Edison and perhaps some notes about him in your work. The private companies were bought up and became part of the Post Office in 1912. You might be able to find out whether there are any places in Britain that still have a privately owned telephone service.

In order to phone in the early days, you had to lift up the receiver and wait until the operator asked you what number you wanted. Then you had to wait again until the operator had connected you. You can see in the picture underneath how

An operator on the Royal Exchange switchboard, Manchester, in 1895

this was done with plugs. If the two plugs were pushed into the correct holes, you and your friend could hear each other; if they were pulled out, you could not.

How the system has grown

Now, of course, most exchanges are fully automatic and many of the smaller ones have no operators; engineers visit them occasionally to see they are working properly. Your local postmaster might help you to find out how many telephones there are now in Great Britain, how many inland calls are made on them each year and how many overseas calls, and you could think of an interesting way of showing this. Perhaps you could compare with the number of telephones and calls on your own local exchange.

In 1970, three out of every ten households had a telephone. The Post Office expects that at least six out of every ten will have one by 1980.

You might be able to find maps showing the telephone network in Britain for various years and make copies of them for your project. At first there were only private telephones and no call-boxes.

The switchroom in the Birmingham Central Exchange in the early years of this century

Improvements in the telephone service

In 1958, H.M. the Queen dialled the first long-distance trunk call from Bristol to Edinburgh. This was the beginning of the Subscriber Trunk Dialling system – generally called S.T.D. Nearly everyone can dial most of his trunk calls now and of course this is not only quicker but also cheaper than having to go through the operator.

International Subscriber Dialling was introduced in 1963 and it became possible to dial a Paris number direct from London. More and more places abroad are being linked up with places in Britain in this way.

Among smaller improvements, hand microphones in various colours are coming into use instead of the old-fashioned kind of receiver. You could illustrate the two kinds side by side, with a caption giving the advantages of the newer kind.

Special services

If you look in the front of your local telephone directory, you will find information that you can use in your project about some special services provided by means of the telephone. Two examples of this are getting the correct time from the speaking clock and getting the latest score when a Test Match is being played. You could think of a good way to illustrate these and other special services.

For people who are physically handicapped or who have difficulty in hearing or seeing or speaking, so that they cannot easily use an ordinary telephone, special devices are now available. You can find out about these from your local telephone sales office.

Overseas telephones

The first telephone conversation across the English Channel took place between London and Paris in March 1891, but it was not until 1923 that it was possible to speak from London to New York across the Atlantic Ocean. In 1925, the Post Office opened a public service for this, but it cost £15 for a three-minute talk. Since then it has gradually become cheaper. It is now possible to speak to someone in New Zealand, which of course is right at the opposite side of the world. You may be able to find out how long this has been possible and how much it now costs.

A map of the world with lines joining London to Paris, New York and Wellington (New Zealand) would be interesting. On the lines you could write the distances between the cities and under the lines the date when it was first possible to have a telephone conversation between them.

Overseas telephone services have been greatly improved by the laying of trans-Atlantic and trans-Pacific telephone cables. 'Repeaters' or amplifiers are now laid about every thirty miles along the cables. These make reception much clearer.

One of the very latest developments has been the opening in London of the first electronic telephone exchange in Europe. By this means it is possible to carry on a trans-Atlantic conversation by bouncing the signals off the Telstar space satellite.

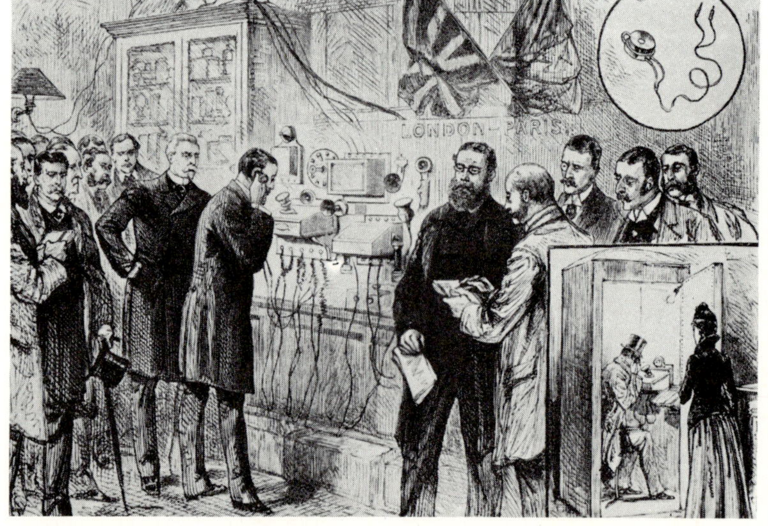

The first telephone call from London to Paris, March 18th, 1891. The London Post Master General speaking to his opposite number in Paris

Telex

Very important telephone conversations are usually confirmed in writing, to make sure there is no mistake or misunderstanding. Telex, another very recent development of the telephone service, sends a spoken message and records it as well. This is a private arrangement between two people. The message is typed on a teleprinter and at the same time recorded in print in the offices of the sender and the recipient. So the Telex message travels as fast as it would by telephone and is as accurate as a written message. One great advantage of Telex is that the teleprinter will operate at any time during the day or night, so long as it is left connected to an electric power supply. There need be no-one in the office where the message is received.

As you know, the time in different parts of the world is different – London time is several hours ahead of New York time, and so on. So the Telex teleprinter can be busy throughout the night making a record of orders and messages from other parts of the world. When the businessman arrives in his office in the morning, the orders and messages are there waiting for him.

Telex has also proved very useful to travel agents in making bookings for holidays abroad.

Datel – sending data by telephone

This is a somewhat similar service to Telex and is particularly useful to shops with a large number of branches. Data, of course, means information – facts and figures. By means of the Datel equipment, information about goods sold and required by each branch shop can be accurately recorded in the head office and so speed up the delivery of the enormous quantities of goods needed by the shops today.

Radio

In its issue of 12 December 1896, the *Westminster Gazette* reported:

> Mr. W. H. Preece, the telegraphic expert of the Post Office, had a surprise in store for his audience at Toynbee Hall on Saturday night, when he lectured on, 'Telegraphy without Wires'. . . . . Towards the end of his lecture he announced that a Mr. Marconi, a young Italian electrician, came to him recently with a system of telegraphy without wires, depending . . . on electric waves . . . of a vibration (of) 250,000,000 a second. These vibrations were projected through space in straight lines . . .

Mr. Marconi was present that night, and this was the first

> occasion on which the apparatus had been shown, except to the Government officials.

It is a little surprising to realize at what an early date overseas communication by wireless became possible. By 1899, wireless messages were being sent across the English Channel and only two years later across the Atlantic Ocean. In 1904, wireless was placed under the control of the government and only the Post Office was allowed to sanction the building of broadcasting stations. No wireless apparatus could be set up in Britain or on a British ship, without a licence from the Postmaster General. You could make a list of reasons why these restrictions were necessary.

It is a sad fact that, when the liner *Titanic* struck an iceberg in the Atlantic in 1912 and almost all her passengers and crew were drowned, there was another ship only twelve miles away, but contact by wireless was not possible. The other ship saw the Titanic's distress signals, but these were flares and the officers of the other ship thought it was a firework display and did not realize the danger the Titanic was in.

Nowadays, the Post Office ship-to-shore radio service provides ships throughout the world with telephone and telegraph facilities.

When war broke out in 1914, any private wireless stations and apparatus were taken over by the Post Office until the end of the war. After that, there was a very rapid growth of wireless and in 1923 the British Broadcasting Corporation was set up under licence from the Post Office.

Here is the account, given in a book published in 1913, of how the Admiralty installed wireless in that year:

> I am told that when Lord Fisher conceived the idea of having wireless telegraphy installed on the cupola of the Admiralty in Whitehall, he found that the Post Office was an insuperable barrier to the scheme. So one day half a dozen seamen swarmed up the cupola and ran up the 'wireless' in the face of outraged authority. 'How's this?' asked the Post Office. 'By whose authority?' And the official breast swelled with official indignation. 'Oh', said the Admiral, 'it's only run up tentatively to see how it will work in case permission is given.' I fancy permission has never been

> given; but if you go down Whitehall, you will see the 'wireless' still audaciously challenging the Post Office proprieties.

We hear a good deal nowadays about traffic congestion in the streets, but a great many people do not realize that there is just as much congestion underground, so that in many places it is quite impossible to lay any more telephone cables. This means that telephone communications must now go through the air instead of under the ground and radio beams are used for this. You can find out more about this in Chapter 7 in the section about the Post Office Tower.

Television

It was in 1925 that the first successful transmission of a picture took place. You could find out who was responsible for this. The first public demonstration of television was in 1936 and this is part of the account of it that appeared next day in the *Morning Post*:

> Yesterday's first demonstration of television over the air from Alexandra Palace at Olympia, London, began in tragic comedy and ended in triumph. First, it appears, a fuse blew at the Palace, a quickly remediable mishap which may befall any piece of technical equipment. At about the same time the electrical equipment at Olympia began to give trouble. The connection of eight viewing booths to a single aerial necessitated amplification. The transformer required refused to work.
>
> The result, half an hour later, was the appearance of a news-reel showing recent happenings in Spain, but liberally bespattered with dancing spots of light. Moreover, only one out of the eight receivers could be used at a time. Then, two hours after the demonstration had been due to begin, we saw real television. We saw a close-up, with the sheen of a woman's hair almost as clearly reflected as in photography. We saw a man in his shirt-sleeves in a studio with a clarity which no previous demonstration had suggested would be possible. We saw dancing and supper table scenes from the film *It's a Girl* with Miss Jessie Matthews as

> sharply portrayed as any critic could wish. Most impressive of all, we saw daylight scenes shot from the balcony of Alexandra Palace in the failing light of 7.45 p.m. on a late August evening.

Now, of course, the Post Office telecommunications system provides sound and television networks for both the B.B.C. and the I.T.V.

You could make good use of illustrations of school broadcasts in your project. If you have pictures of the first landing of men on the moon, they would fit in well, too. Space travel, of course, has only become possible with the use of radio and television. Another new Post Office service, using closed circuit television, which you could ask about, is called 'Confravision'.

Postage stamps 6

Before adhesive postage stamps

Materials for stamps – paper, gum, ink

The first British stamps

Modern stamps

The advantage of using stamps

Before adhesive postage stamps

It is surprising to find a stamp mentioned as long ago as 1661, almost 200 years before Rowland Hill's time. In that year, Colonel Henry Bishop, the Postmaster General, wrote:

> A stamp is invented that is put upon every letter showing the day of the moneth that every letter comes to the office, so that no Letter Carryer may dare to detayne a letter from post to post, which before was usual.

This was in fact a circular date-stamp, put on by hand. What is the modern name for this?

As a matter of fact, Bishop himself had been responsible for a good deal of the delay he complained about. He was rather like the famous Vicar of Bray in the way he changed sides. He fought as a Royalist in the Civil War, but when the King's army was defeated in 1644 he fled abroad. Two years later, he returned to England, took the oath of allegiance to Cromwell, and was made Postmaster General. At that time, the Post Office was full of Puritan spies and informers. Letters sent through the post by Royalists were shamelessly opened by them. If there was anything that could possibly be made to look like treachery, it would be reported to the authorities, the writer would be punished and the informer rewarded.

Although Bishop is usually called, 'the father of the postmark', at least two earlier postmarks are known. One was stamped in Milan in 1459 and the other was on a letter sent to the painter, Leonardo da Vinci, in 1519.

For his London postal service, William Dockwra used a simple triangular postmark, stamped on by hand, which said, 'Penny Post Paid'. You could find a drawing of this and make a copy of it.

Materials for stamps

Look closely at a postage stamp and decide what are the three chief materials used. They are the same today as in 1840, but each has changed a good deal in the meantime.

1 *Paper*

The first machinery for making paper was set up at Frogmore in Hampshire in 1803, but most of the early stamps were printed on hand-made paper. This was made in a paper-mould, a wooden frame with two other frames, one of which had fine wire cloth stretched across it. If you can find a picture of a paper-mould, you can mount it and write a caption to explain how it was used. Nowadays, almost all paper is machine-made.

The first stamps, in 1840, were printed on hand-made deckle-edged paper made only by Stacey Wise at the Rush Mills, Hardington, Northants. If you live anywhere near there, you could find out whether these mills still exist.

The government supervised the making of the paper for stamps very strictly. Only the exact amount needed for each printing was issued to the printers and they had to show any spoiled sheets to the government inspectors. If a sheet was missing, they had to pay what the stamps on that sheet would have been worth. You can think why 240 stamps were printed on each sheet. How many stamps are there on a sheet now that decimal money has come into use?

Water marks

If you hold a pound note up to the light, you will see that the white part has a pattern in it. This is a watermark and proves that the note is a genuine one. To prevent forgery, the paper used for making stamps had a special watermark, too. This mark was made by sewing or welding small bits of wire on to the wire cloth in the paper-mould.

2 *Ink*
The printers of the early stamps ground up their own colours and mixed them with a varnish made from linseed oil, resin and soap. They sometimes added tallow, to make the ink more greasy. At that time, stamps were printed in one colour only.

3 *Gum*
In the margins of the first sheets of stamps, there was a warning, 'In wetting the back be careful not to remove the Cement.' This 'cement' was ordinary potato-flour paste. If the sheets of stamps got very hot, the gummed side shrank and made the edges of the sheets curl up. In a damp climate, the sheets stuck together and could not be pulled apart without damaging the stamps.
A great improvement was the use of gum Arabic. The gum was smeared on with a brush and the sheets were then hung up to dry. Even this improved gum had its drawbacks: it was difficult to gum the sheets evenly and they were awkward to handle because they curled up so badly after the gum was dry. If gum Arabic is used nowadays, the gummed paper is passed through a machine that breaks up the film of gum into tiny scales.
Recently, a plastic adhesive called P.V.A. (Polyvinyl Alcohol) has taken the place of gum Arabic. This can be applied to the stamps much more easily and quickly. It is almost invisible and has no taste or smell.

The first British stamps

You will remember that it was Rowland Hill who suggested the use of adhesive stamps, but actually a postage stamp had been designed in 1834 by a printer and bookseller called James Chalmers, who lived in Dundee. This stamp was never used, probably because it had been printed in a way that would have made it easy to forge copies of it. Instead, the head of Queen Victoria was printed on the first pictorial stamps in the world issued on 1 May 1840 – the Penny Black and the Twopence Blue.

The first pictorial postage stamps ever issued

These first stamps were printed from cut steel plates. In making the first plate, the engraver, Charles Heath, worked for five days on the Queen's eye alone. The whole picture took several weeks to complete. Once photography had come into use, sketches or photographs could be reproduced mechanically instead of having to be drawn by hand. A hand-press was used in printing the first stamps. The edges were not perforated, so the stamps had to be cut from the sheet with scissors or a sharp knife.

Modern stamps

A modern stamp-factory uses machine-made paper, ink and gum, and machines are used for printing, perforating and gumming the stamps and even for engraving the design – for everything, in fact, except thinking out the design.

Only a few firms print stamps. For example, Bradbury Wilkinson & Co. Ltd print those that cost from 10p to £1, while Harrison's of High Wycombe print those costing less than 10p. Unfortunately, it is very difficult to get permission from the Post Office to visit these factories, but you will realize why this is necessary. Harrison's have eighteen Post Office workers as supervisors. They work in shifts, so that there are always some on duty. Apart from supervising the work, where necessary, these inspectors are responsible for collecting and counting any faulty sheets of stamps and burning them in a burglar-proof incinerator. If one stamp on a sheet is faulty, the whole sheet is destroyed.

Designing and printing stamps today

This is quite a complicated business. Suggestions for new stamps are sent in to the Post Office by all kinds of people. The Council of Industrial Design sends in the names of artists who are good at drawing the very small kind of designs needed for stamps. When the kinds of stamps have been chosen, and also the artists, each artist sends in a design, four times larger than the stamp will be. The most suitable design is sent to the printers, so that they can make a sample stamp in full colour. This has to be approved, first by the Post Office and then by the Queen herself.

You may have noticed the little spots of colour along the edges of sheets of stamps and wondered what they are for. Now

A set of four beautifully designed stamps

that most stamps are printed in several colours, these spots are useful when the sheets are being checked. The examiners can see that all the colours have been printed correctly.

Modern British stamps are overprinted with a band of phosphorus, so that letters can be sorted and handled electronically. Your science teacher would be able to tell you more about this.

An interesting set of four stamps that you could probably get and use for illustrating this section of your work, would be those issued on 1 October 1969, to mark the change from the General

One of the set of four stamps issued to commemorate the setting up of the Post Office Corporation

Post Office to the Post Office Corporation. They show some of the most recent and interesting developments in the Post Office, such as the national Giro service and automatic letter-sorting.

Advantages of using postage stamps

You could make a list of these advantages: saving a special journey to the Post Office, . . . and so forth. Actually, the greatest advantage was that letters no longer had to be handled to decide what fee was due and so there was no excuse for prying into them and people felt, for the first time, that they could write freely to their friends.

Post Offices 7

The need for a special building

Good and bad Post Offices

Services provided at a modern Post Office

The need for a special Post Office building
You will remember that at first the whole postal service consisted of messengers who collected the letters and delivered them. At that time, of course, no special building was needed.

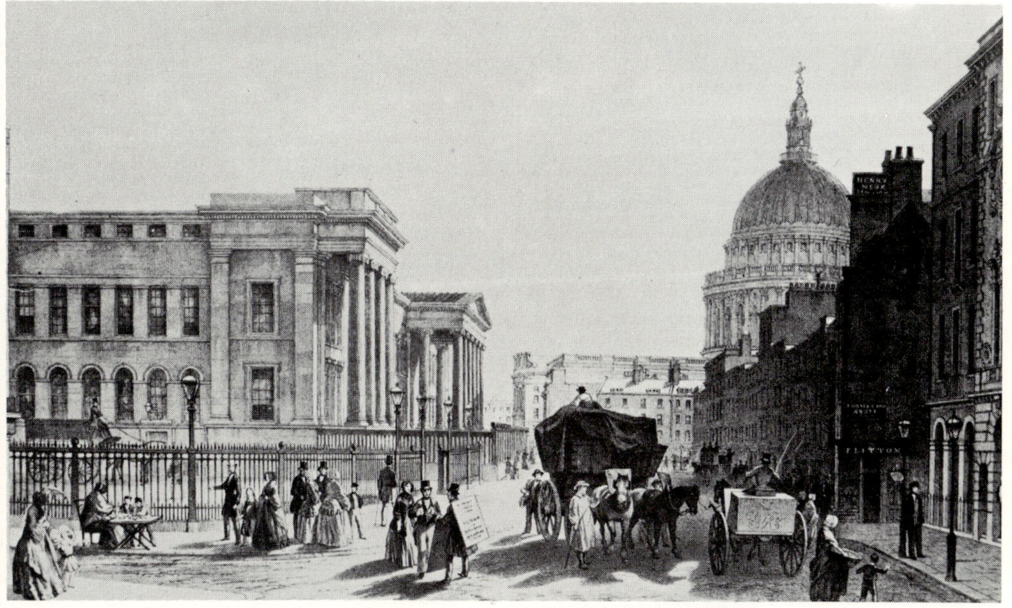

The General Post Office, London, 1852. Notice a mail van and other vehicles, and the dress of the time

As more and more letters were being sent, someone was needed to plan and supervise the work of the messengers, and these overseers were called post 'masters'. The first postmasters were innkeepers, as well. You could make a list of reasons why this was a good idea and perhaps sketch one of the early postmasters with a mug of ale in one hand and a bundle of letters in the other. This could be a painting, drawing, or an appliqué figure.

As you read on in this chapter, you could make a series of drawings of Post Office buildings, starting with nothing at all – just a cross, perhaps – then an inn, and so on. Or you could collect actual photographs.

As the postal service expanded, there were records to be kept. How many kinds can you think of? So, even before people had to go to the Post Office to buy stamps, some kind of office had become necessary.

Different kinds of Post Offices now

If you have ever lived right out in the country, or perhaps spent your holidays there, you will know that, even today, the Post Office may be just a small part of the village shop. On the other hand, some towns are now so large that, as well as a local Post Office in each area, there are district Post Offices, each one in charge of several local offices. You could think out just what the work of these district offices must be. If you live in a town, it will be easy to talk to somebody who works there and find out whether you have thought of everything. If you live in the country, you would need to check from books or when you

The special Post Office at Wembley Stadium during the Olympic Games, 1948

are visiting a town, or your local postmaster or postmistress may be able to help you.

The Post Office is now so large that its headquarters in London occupy several large buildings. Many departments have their headquarters in the City, in or near what used to be called the General Post Office. It is now known as the London Chief Office. There are also important offices in the West End, near the Post Office Tower.

The Post Office Tower

This very modern Post Office building in London is well worth a visit. There are sometimes nearly a million visitors a year, and you may have to wait some time in a queue, but while you are waiting or moving slowly along, you will find the charts on the walls well worth studying.

If you are over fourteen years of age, the admission fee is 20p; for children under fourteen it is 10p, but they are only admitted with an adult. You can buy an illustrated handbook, postcards, special stamps and a cut-out model of the Tower that would all be useful in your project. Be sure to take your notebook – there is a machine that automatically answers a great many questions about the tower. You could find out, for instance, how long it took to build and when it came into use.

The Post Office Tower is the tallest building in Britain today and is more than 200 feet taller than any other London building. We have seen that telephone communications must now go

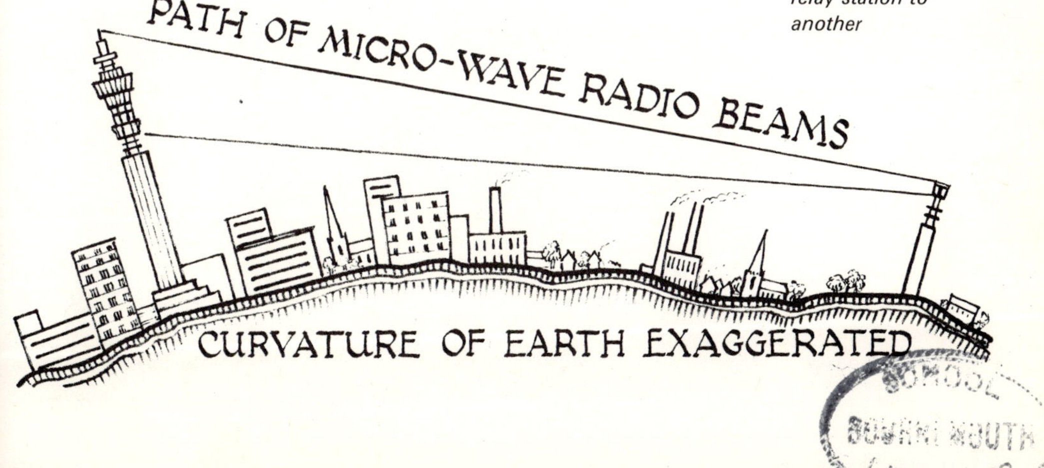

How micro-wave radio beams travel from one relay station to another

through the air, rather than underground, and the same is true for television. Micro-wave radio beams are used. These waves travel in straight lines, so relay-stations have to be built at intervals to carry the beams round the earth's curved surface, as you can see in the diagram. The beams must be able to keep clear of even the tallest buildings. This accounts for the great height of the Tower, but do you see any dangers that might threaten it? The engineers needed to build a very high tower, but they had to make it safe and they wanted it to look well. If you make a model or a sketch of the Post Office Tower as part of your project, you could use it to stress these points.

Good and bad Post Offices – outside

You will almost certainly be visiting a number of Post Offices while you are working on your project. If you look carefully at the building before you go in, you will notice how different they are from each other. Is yours modern or older? Is it bright and clean-looking, or drab? Is it well placed in the town or village? Could a stranger find it easily? What about the lettering on the outside?

As you go into the Post Office, notice whether the door is convenient. Is it too narrow, so that you have to wait for people

Wallingford Post Office has the monogram of Edward VIII carved over its doorway

to come out before you can go in? Should there perhaps be more entrances than there are? Would a different kind of door make things easier? A great many people use the Post Offices every day, so these are important points.

Good and bad Post Offices – inside

Look round critically as you go in. Is the lighting good? Is there room to move about, without colliding with other people? Can people get what they want without waiting very long? If the Post Office has been well planned, you will feel that it is a pleasant yet businesslike place, and you will find several things that help to make it so: the colours and materials used on walls, floors and ceilings, the lights, the counters and other fittings, whether it is neither too hot nor too chilly, and so on. Next, look carefully at the notices on the walls and the various printed forms. Are they displayed so that it is easy to find the one you want? Is there a case of interesting stamps, or a display of books of stamps? Look at them carefully, to see whether you think they make the Post Office more interesting and useful.

Are there comfortable quarters for the staff? a sitting room? cooking facilities? first aid? lavatories? These are important points which you could find out about in a conversation with one of the clerks when he, or she, is not too busy.

You could have one section of your project called something like 'A good modern Post Office'. It would be a good idea if you could make large clear sketches of the exterior and interior of your ideal Post Office and label them so as to stress the points that make them attractive and at the same time suitable for their purpose. This would be far more striking than just describing a good Post Office. You could discuss with your domestic science or art teacher what colours are suitable for a public building, which are cheerful, which show the dirt quickly, and so on.

Services provided by a modern Post Office

Here again it will be worth your while to think of an interesting way of showing the various services provided, rather than just making a list of them. We have already discussed the postal services and telecommunications. These are the most important services the Post Office provides today, but there are a great many others.

Money orders and postal orders

You can well imagine that in the early days of the postal services it would have been extremely risky to send money through the post. Coins and even bank notes would very likely have been 'lost'. So it was as early as 1838 that money orders were introduced and these are still in use today.

Postal orders were introduced in 1883. At first, they were called postal notes and they could be issued for any sum of money up to £1. You could find out whether this is still the case.

Both money orders and postal orders have a counterfoil that you can fill in and keep, to show when you posted the order. What can you do as an extra precaution against theft? When you buy the orders, you pay an extra fee, called poundage. You can check the reasons for the names counterfoil and poundage in a dictionary or encyclopaedia.

The National Giro Service

Since 1968, Giro has provided a new and simple way to pay certain bills. The national boards for gas, electricity, etc., as well as other large concerns like insurance companies, building societies, hire purchase companies and large stores, have Giro accounts. Anyone who has to pay a bill to one of these bodies can fill in a simple slip, which is then sent to the National Giro Centre and the proper amount of money is credited to the right person or company and deducted from the bank balance of the person paying it. Most of the arithmetic connected with Giro accounts is done by computers. It is expected that, in course of time, a great many private people will have Giro accounts and so make the service even more useful. Can you find out why Giro is so called?

The Savings Bank

A great many young children have a Savings Bank account

started for them by their parents or a friend. Anyone can open a Savings Bank account by going to a Post Office and paying in 25p or more. You are really lending your money to the government, so every £1 in your account earns some interest each year. Many older people like to put some of their money into this Bank, although they know they could get more interest elsewhere. They know their money is quite safe because the government guarantees it. It is also quite quick and easy to take your money out when you want to. If you need £20 or less, you just take your book to the Post Office and fill in a slip to say how much you want. You could find out what happens if you want to take out more than £20.

The Post Office Savings Bank was started in 1861. In 1880, the Postmaster General, Henry Fawcett, was keen to encourage children and the poorer people of the time to save what little money they could. This of course was before the introduction of decimal money, so he issued slips on to which twelve penny stamps could be stuck, rather like the pages in the National

'Ernie'

Savings books now. At that time, a Post Office savings account could be started with one shilling. So, when the slip was full, it could be taken to the Post Office and used to start an account.

Post Office sales

Apart from postage stamps, there are four main groups of things sold at Post Offices:

1 National Savings' stamps, Premium Bonds, and other government bonds. (What are bonds?)
2 Licences for a dog, for T.V., radio. . . . How many more can you find out about?
3 National Insurance stamps.
4 Stationery already stamped – letter-cards, postcards, envelopes and air-letters. It would be interesting to find out which of these are sometimes sold from automatic machines.

Actual examples of some of these things the Post Office sells would make this section of your project more interesting.

Pensions and allowances

These are paid by the government, so it was easy to arrange that they could be claimed at Post Offices. You could make sketches of typical people getting this money from the Post Office and so show what these payments are for – retirement pensions, family allowances and so forth.

So far we have been considering the work of the Post Office. In the next chapter we shall be thinking about the workers, who run the Post Office services.

Post Office workers 8

Postmasters in the past

Postmasters today – in London and in other regions

Other workers – postmen, telephonists, counter-clerks and engineers

Getting a job in the Post Office – working conditions

Women workers in the Post Office

The early postmasters

We have seen that the first postmasters were royal officials and that, as the postal services expanded, postmasters were needed to organize and supervise them. Before the days of postage stamps, the postmasters had also to collect the fees that had to be paid for sending a letter.

As innkeepers, the first duty of the early postmasters was to have horses and accommodation ready for officials and messengers travelling on the king's business. It is easy to see how this fitted in with their job as postmaster as well.

A certain Mr Hobson, a postmaster in Cambridgeshire, always insisted that his horses should be let out strictly in order. The traveller, whoever he might be, must take the horse nearest the stable door, or go without. It is from this that the expression 'Hobson's choice' is still used to mean that one has no choice at all. You could illustrate an angry traveller trying to break Mr Hobson's rule.

Postmasters as newspaper owners

When messengers arrived and reported to the postmaster, they would naturally also pass on any news they had picked up on the way. It was easy for the postmasters to write down this news and pass it on. Thus it happened that in most places, both in Europe and America, the first editors and owners of newspapers were the postmasters.

Later postmasters

As the British postal service expanded, branch offices were established in various places, in addition to the main one in London. These were in charge of sub-postmasters. Later, these men were called postmasters, while their chief in London became the Postmaster General. This lasted until the Post Office became a Corporation in 1969. You could find out what the head of the Post Office is now called – and who he is. As the services supplied by the Post Office became more numerous and varied, the Postmasters needed more and more

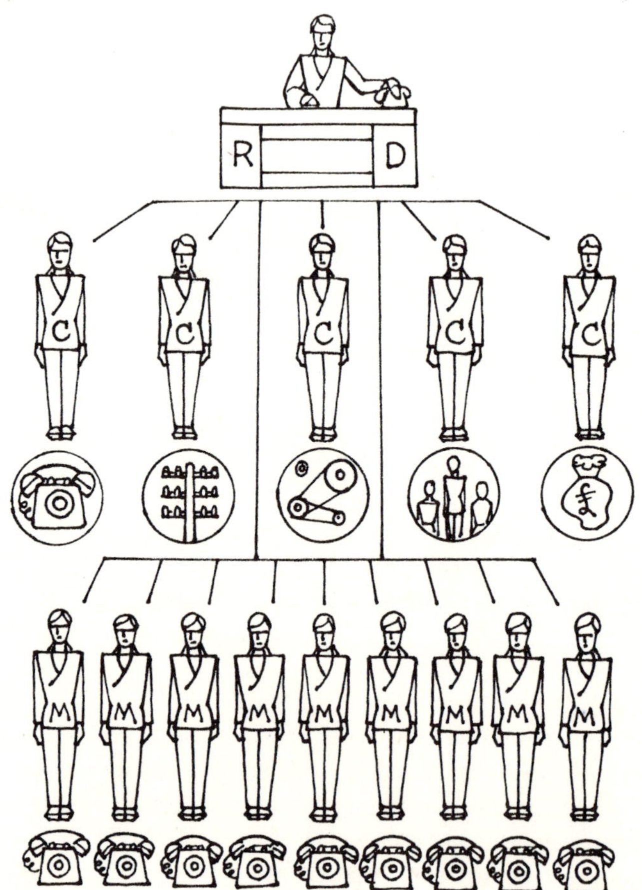

Staff in charge of the London Telecommunications Region

assistants, so that the Post Office is now a very large and complicated organization.

London postmasters

London is now so huge that the London postal region is divided into an inner area and an outer area. The inner area is a circle stretching about six or seven miles in every direction from the centre. Seven district postmasters are responsible for this area. The outer area is a belt about ten miles wide outside the inner area, with seventeen head postmasters in charge of it. A coloured diagram of the inner and outer areas and their postmasters would make this part of your work interesting.

The chart opposite shows the links between the regional director, the controllers and managers.

Postal divisions

The country is divided into ten postal regions. These are:

Region	*Headquarters in*
1 London	London
2 Midland	Birmingham
3 North Eastern	Leeds
4 North Western	Manchester
5 Northern Ireland	Belfast
6 Scotland	Edinburgh
7 South Western	Bristol
8 Wales and the Marches	Cardiff
9 Eastern	Colchester
10 South Eastern	Brighton

You could mark these towns on an outline map of Britain and think of an interesting way to show the postal regions that have their headquarters in each of them. Notice which region you live in and find out your postal district and telephone area. Where could you get in touch with your head postmaster and telephone manager?

Other Post Office workers today

The Post Office Corporation now employs more than 400,000 people. Many of these are postmen, telephone operators or the clerks who serve at Post Office counters. In addition, there are a large number of engineers, who design and produce the equipment and cables needed for telephone, telegraph and radio services.

Postmen

It is possible to go straight from school to work as a postman. At first, the boy-postmen will deliver telegrams or act as indoor messengers. They may deliver the telegrams on foot or use a bicycle; when they are old enough, they may be taught to ride a motor-cycle. Their messenger work may be in a telephone manager's office or some other Post Office department. Within this office, they will collect and deliver the letters and see that everyone has the stationery they need. They may sometimes help in such way as making tea for the office staff, but at the same time they will be learning their job. As time goes on, they will work more and more at collecting, sorting and delivering letters. By the time they are eighteen, they may be carrying out all the duties of an adult postman. Pin-figure sketches showing the jobs a young postman does would be fun to do and would add interest to your project.

Conditions for postmen today are much pleasanter than in the past. There is still in existence a letter written to the Postmaster General last century to ask 'whether anything can be done for a cycle-postman who has ridden through the seat of his trousers'. He got a new pair! Now, of course, their uniforms are provided for them, as well as their bicycles (if they use them), and they can claim a meal-voucher towards the cost of a hot meal every day. As well as this, young postmen are encouraged to attend special classes one day a week during working hours. This is not only to help them in their work, but also to carry on their education, so that they have the best possible chance in life. Of course their pay is much better now, too, and they are paid for their holidays. On the other hand, postmen often have to start work very early in the morning and of course they are out in all kinds of weather. You could find out how many hours a week they are expected to work and whether they always work the same hours.

Telephonists

Most people think of telephone operators sitting at a switchboard putting through calls that the subscribers cannot dial for themselves. You could write down – or illustrate – the other jobs they have to do. Telephone calls have to be paid for, so the telephonist must keep a record of the calls that are made. Perhaps you could find out exactly how this is done. You could find out, too, how dialled calls are recorded. Then you could make two contrasting illustrations of the telephone operator, one working at the switchboard and the other working elsewhere at the various jobs connected with the making-up of subscribers' accounts, sorting and pricing the tickets that are used for this.

Sometimes, too, the operators may be dealing with Directory inquiries or with 999 emergency calls or with the testing of switchboard equipment. It would obviously be useful to visit a telephone exchange before you make your illustrations. Your teacher might arrange to take a group of you, or he could tell you how to make your own arrangements.

A supervisor checking one of the tickets on which STD telephone calls are recorded

Postal and telegraph officers

This is what clerks who serve at Post Office counters are officially called. They deal with all the activities of a modern Post Office that we have mentioned earlier – selling stamps and postal orders, paying out pensions and allowances, dealing with parcels and telegrams and so forth. At other times, they may work behind the scenes, as it were, in a Head Post Office. You could make a list of the jobs you think they do there, many of them connected with answering inquiries and with keeping the accounts for all the business that goes on in the Post Offices. Here again, you could make two contrasted illustrations to show the two sides of their work.

How to get a job in the Post Office

You could look in your local paper and in the Post Office or elsewhere to find advertisements for jobs as postmen, telephonists, counter clerks or engineers. The advertisements will probably tell you how old you must be if you wish to apply, whether you need any special qualifications and so on. If you collect a number of these advertisements, you could mount them as part of your project and so provide accurate information about Post Office work in your area. You might even think of applying for one of these jobs when you leave school.

There would be good prospects of promotion, because usually only those who are already Post Office workers can become supervisors and managers in the Post Office. This does not mean that if you started as a telephonist, say, you would always work with telephones. Postal workers have a wide choice. If you wanted to, you could apply for promotion to a higher post in a different department.

Training schemes

Post Office workers are all fully trained for their work. They do not have to pay for this training and there are special schemes to help those who wish to change over to a different kind of work in the Post Office.

Other advantages

Post Office workers today have their own staff associations and quite a lot of say in Post Office affairs. There are so many of them that they can arrange all kinds of sports and other activities for themselves. There are links with Post Office workers in other countries, too, which may lead to travel and to interesting friendships.

In the Post Office, there is a very long tradition of service to the community. All its workers are concerned with putting people in touch with each other in one or other of the many ways that are possible today.

Some disadvantages

Successful workers in the Post Office may find that, several times in their career, they have to move their homes to another area because they have to go and work there. Some people, of course, quite enjoy these changes, but others may not. A more serious drawback is that some senior staff have to spend some years on travelling duties. This means that sometimes they will have to spend several nights each week away from home. Most of them find, however, that they enjoy their job enough to be willing to put up with this.

You could sketch a postman, or another kind of Post Office worker, being pulled forward by the advantages he enjoys and dragged backwards by the disadvantages of his job. You should make it clear whether in the end he is moving forward or backward!

Postwomen

Not many women or girls were employed by the Post Office until this century, but there is a record that 'Mary Jackson took the mails every day from 1819 to 1870, walking a total of 250,000 miles'. About how many miles a year was this? And how many miles every day, in all weathers? How would you have liked her job, for very little pay?

By 1939, there were quite a number of postmistresses, especially in country districts, and at least 600 postwomen. As more and more men were called up for war work during the Second

World War, their places were taken by women, so that by the end of the war in 1945 there were 20,000 postwomen and even 3,000 women telephone engineers, as well as large numbers of sorters, counter-clerks and van-drivers.

Women telephonists

From the beginning of the service, telephone operators were nearly all women. Before the Second World War, there was a rule that women must resign their posts if they got married, but by 1942 telephonists were so badly needed that the Post Office was appealing to married telephonists 'to come back and lend a hand at the switchboards'. What is the rule now? You might find out how many men and how many women telephone operators there are in your own district now and whether they do the same work as each other.

Other people who work for the Post Office

A great many people now work for the Post Office, although they are not directly employed by the Post Office Corporation. For example, a great deal of printing has to be done. You could collect and mount different kinds of stamps – postage, savings', etc. – pages from the Post Office Guide and from a telephone directory, as well as examples of Post Office forms.

The future 9

Automation

Expansion

Staff

Automation

We have seen that automation is spreading throughout the Post Office services and there is no doubt that it will continue to do so, but there is a limit. The postman's task has been made easier by various automatic devices, but it seems highly improbable that the postman himself will ever be replaced by a robot who will walk up to our houses and put the letters in the box!

In the same way, the routine work in telephone exchanges will be more and more carried out automatically, but there will still be special services that will need a *person* to deal with them – perhaps you can think of examples. Automatic exchanges, too, will continue to need to be inspected periodically.

Expansion

Some of Britain's telephones still use letters as well as figures in dialling. The spread of all-figure numbers will be a great aid to the dialling of international calls, since almost all other countries now use figures only. It is expected that, by the end of the century, there will be twenty million telephones in Britain and in most cases it will be possible to dial direct to any place in the world.

The British telecommunications system is now the third largest in the world. It is easy to think which two countries have larger systems. By 1980, it is expected that there will be twice as many telephone connections in Britain, that the Telex system will be five times as large, and that there will be at least twenty times as many data transmission terminals.

Research

At the Post Office research station at Dollis Hill in north-west London, experiments are being carried out on various ways of expanding telecommunications. The workers there are trying, too, to improve the efficiency of the micro-wave links that are being set up all over the country.

Work is already under way to develop a new type of communications link, which would carry 400,000 telephone conversations at the same time, or 200 colour television channels. This will be done by means of 'waveguides'. These pipes, two inches in diameter, will carry transmissions at very high radio frequencies. In time, these will develop into a kind of 'communications motorway' system to handle the vast telecommunications traffic expected in the future.

Through its 'tracking station' at Goonhilly Down in Cornwall, the Post Office already maintains telecommunications and television links by satellite with eighteen countries.

An experimental model of an electronic telephone exchange, 1969

Innovations

Within sixty years, according to the *Telecommunications Journal*, telephone services will be built into houses in the same way as water, gas and electricity are now. It will become quite usual to have several telephones in a house, forming its own 'inter-com' system, and a telephone in the car.

Television telephones will make the callers visible to each other. Television aerials will no longer be needed. The only remaining ones are likely to be community ones, receiving broadcasts direct from satellites like Telstar.

Staff

The change-over to being an independent Corporation has given the Post Office freedom to develop on its own lines, so that it has become more like an ordinary business enterprise. This, of course, has made a difference to the attitude of the Post Office to its workers, and vice versa.

Although automation will reduce the number of workers needed, the vast expansion of services that is anticipated will call for more staff. Many more of these than in the past will need to be engineers and scientists. So in the future the Post Office will look to the universities and to polytechnics and technical colleges for many of its staff.

Each year the Post Office now offers about fifty university studentships in communications, engineering and science. Holders of these studentships go to university at the expense of the Post Office. They also receive a salary and in the long vacations they gain practical experience by working in a Post Office. Usually it is also arranged for them to work for a time in a Post Office abroad. A far cry indeed from the early days of the Post Office!

By the time you have completed your project, you will know something about the history and organization of the Post Office and about the opportunities for workers in the Post Office today. More important, your project will have helped you to a better understanding of the modern world in which we live.

Acknowledgments

The author and publishers would like to thank those listed below for permission to reproduce illustrations:

Crown Agents Stamp Bureau, photographs by Courtesy of the Post Office, photograph of 'Ernie' by Courtesy of the Director of Savings.

The author wishes to thank the members of the staff of the Publicity Department of the Post Office for their very willing co-operation in securing photographs.